Death of a Ventriloquist

Previous Winners of the Vassar Miller Prize in Poetry
Scott Cairns, Founding Editor
John Poch, Series Editor

Partial Eclipse by Tony Sanders
Selected by Richard Howard

Delirium by Barbara Hamby
Selected by Cynthia Macdonald

The Sublime by Jonathan Holden
Selected by Yusef Komunyakaa

American Crawl by Paul Allen
Selected by Sydney Lea

Soul Data by Mark Svenvold
Selected by Heather McHugh

Moving & St rage by Kathy Fagan
Selected by T. R. Hummer

A Protocol for Touch by Constance Merritt
Selected by Eleanor Wilner

The Perseids by Karen Holmberg
Selected by Sherod Santos

The Self as Constellation by Jeanine Hathaway
Selected by Madeline DeFrees

Bene-Dictions by Rush Rankin
Selected by Rosanna Warren

Losing and Finding by Karen Fiser
Selected by Lynne McMahon

The Black Beach by J. T. Barbarese
Selected by Andrew Hudgins

re-entry by Michael White
Selected by Paul Mariani

The Next Settlement by Michael Robins
Selected by Anne Winters

Mister Martini by Richard Carr
Selected by Naomi Shihab Nye

Ohio Violence by Alison Stine
Selected by Eric Pankey

Stray Home by Amy M. Clark
Selected by Beth Ann Fennelly

Circles Where the Head Should Be by Caki Wilkinson
Selected by J. D. McClatchy

Death of a Ventriloquist

poems by

Gibson Fay-LeBlanc

2011 Winner, Vassar Miller Prize in Poetry

University of North Texas Press
Denton, Texas

10 9 8 7 6 5 4 3 2 1

Permissions:
University of North Texas Press
1155 Union Circle #311336
Denton, TX 76203-5017

The paper used in this book meets the minimum requirements of the
American National Standard for Permanence of Paper for Printed Library
Materials, z39.48.1984. Binding materials have been chosen for durability.

Library of Congress Cataloging-in-Publication Data
Fay-LeBlanc, Gibson, 1974-
Death of a ventriloquist : poems / by Gibson Fay-LeBlanc. -- 1st ed.
p. cm. -- (Number 19 in the
Vassar Miller prize in poetry series)
Includes bibliographical references.
2011 Winner, Vassar Miller Prize in Poetry
ISBN 978-1-57441-447-9 (pbk. : alk. paper)
ISBN 978-1-57441-455-4 (e-book)
1. Fatherhood--Poetry. 2. Ventriloquists--Poetry. 3.
Ventriloquism--Poetry. I. Title. II. Series: Vassar Miller prize in
poetry series ; no. 19.
PS3606.A953D43 2012
811'.6--dc23
2011042003

Death of a Ventriloquist is Number 19 in the
Vassar Miller Prize in Poetry Series

Cover and interior image by Paul Klee (1879–1940) © 2011 Artists Rights
Society (ARS), New York / VG Bild-Kunst, Bonn. "Ventriloquist and
Crier in the Moor," 1923. Watercolor and transferred printing ink on
paper, bordered with ink, H. 15-1/4 W. 11 inches (38.7x27.9 cm).
The Berggruen Klee Collection, 1984 (1984.315.35).
Image copyright © The Metropolitan Museum of Art.
Image source: Art Resource, NY.

Cover Design: Tammy Ackerman and Joshua Bodwell at North40Creative

For Renée

Contents

Acknowledgments

Grateful acknowledgment is made to the editors of the magazines in which versions of these poems first appeared:

32 Poems: "The Origin of Pigeons" and "The Worst First Line"; *Agenda* (UK): "Caravaggio's Peter"; *Agni Online:* "Explanation Beginning with a River"; *Backwards City Review:* "Rider Unhorsed" and "Months Later the Lawyer Returned" from "A Brief History of the Decline"; *Bellevue Literary Review:* "Worry Bone"; *Blackbird:* "Inspiration," "Ventriloquist on an Off Day," and "Ventriloquist on the Moor"; *Borderlands: Texas Poetry Review:* "Still Life, Young Woman at the Water's Edge"; *Guernica:* "Visiting Chicago"; *Linebreak:* "More Matter, Less Art"; *Maine Magazine:* "Proof #4"; *Poetry Northwest:* "On Leaving Home"; *Prairie Schooner:* "American Beech" and "Learning to Wait"; *Tin House:* "Four Planes of Experience"; *The Café Review:* "Guide" and "Panic Grass and Feverfew"; *The New Republic:* "Oakland Work Crew"; *Southeast Review:* "The Largest of the Circus Animals"; *Western Humanities Review:* "Phaëton"; *Words and Images:* "How to Make Fatherhood Lyrical," "Maker," "Notes on Thirty Years in the Life of a Ventriloquist," and "The Nots."

"American Beech," "Inspiration," "Learning to Wait," "More Matter, Less Art," "Oakland Work Crew," and "Ventriloquist on the Moor" also appear on fishousepoems.org, an audio archive of work by emerging poets.

"On Leaving Home" was *Poetry Northwest's* online feature for December 2007. "Rider Unhorsed" also appeared on Verse Daily for March 16, 2006. "Worry Bone" was awarded the *Bellevue Literary Review's* 2006 Magliocco Prize for Poetry.

"Four Planes of Experience" also appears in *Satellite Convulsions* (Tin House Books).

"Oakland Work Crew" also appears in *From the Fishouse: An Anthology of Poems that Sing, Rhyme, Resound, Syncopate, Alliterate, and Just Plain Sound Great* (Persea).

A number of the poems here appear in *Gaps in the Record*, a signed and numbered limited edition chapbook (Warren Machine, 2008).

Thanks to the Maine Arts Commission, which supported one major revision of this work.

A mountain of gratitude goes to all of my teachers, including Christopher Merrill, whose undergraduate class changed my life, and Eamon Grennan, Marie Howe, Richard Howard, Lucie Brock-Broido, Glyn Maxwell, and Timothy Donnelly, for each providing wonderful and different examples of how to work and make poems.

Thanks to Lisa Russ Spaar and John Poch, who saw that this was a book, and to the folks at University of North Texas Press for making it happen.

Thanks to the many friends and fellow writers who took hammer and chisel to my work and provided encouragement along the way: Craig Teicher, Jesse Ball, Kevin Gonzalez, Keetje Kuipers, Patty Hagge, Jeffrey Thomson, and my longtime brother-in-writing, John Kovatch.

And thanks also to my family, actual and adopted. To the writers, artists, and good people who are part of The Telling Room—thank you for inspiring me for more than five years.

And to Renée, who believed even when I didn't. And to Liam and Emmett, who shape my days. I hope you read this someday.

1

Rider Unhorsed

First reeds at the pathside became vocal
then the dunes' curve met the curvature
inside my eye. I saw Polaris become

five-pointed, and red pines closed the sky
as bluebells opened it. This is vision country.

As to where my horse is, my steed of good
deeds and satchel of bad lemons, or how

my head became a tuning fork in a thicket,
I'm too busy to answer. The alder's summer

is speckled and short-stalked; the blackbird
parades its reds; nuthatches dangle down.

Linger with me; step out of your swivet.
Be mind-muddied a while, and temple-robbed.
Be lullabied by the music of far-off bells.

On Leaving Home

We all need exile once
in a while: actual
or inner, no matter.

We need to be far
from what matters, what-
ever is the matter.

To be clear, the former
and the latter have to do
with the mother and the timber

from which we're made. I,
for one, have elms—for
forts, for sprinting under—

at my center, meaning
also Dutch Elm and canker.
As for the mother, she did

what she could and did
despite the weather:
the gray light, the cloud cover.

I was a foreigner
in a print Neverland
at first; only later

was it actual: new
cities, new coasts. Nowhere,
of course, was I able

to forget the fretted agate
clouds and anvil shapes
of matter, mother and weather.

Guide

She led me in among the voiceless things.
A long hallway, of course, and locked doors.
She asked me to describe their pins and springs.

Some glittered, some were bone; others clung
to jambs on chains: padlocks of flesh, of coral.
She led me quietly, with cunning, and sang

tunelessly, asked of the contents and tongues
she heard shifting behind the veins of mortar.
I asked her what she knew of hidden things.

I said, The mechanisms are mystifying,
the tumblers keyless: they're best left unforced.
She asked me to describe a latch, a spring.

I said, This vault's old, see the patterning
on the lock? A child's scratchings: a hex to ward
off those led in among the voiceless things.

And she: It's just a door, push it, let it spring—
how else to know what's in there so long stored?
I let her in among my voiceless things—
pins in my hands, I began remembering.

The Largest of the Circus Animals

Nights when the heat in my room has mass
and scale, a heft, or I catch a whiff of straw

and dung covered with a dabble of cologne,
I know it looms in a corner with a boy

who can smile at anything. In its stomach is
a quiet house: a family in five red rooms—

five three-legged chairs, five doors shut,
five mouths that never speak of the smell.

I can tell you there are two tusks and a trunk
that plays the role of hand, nose, or snorkel,

depending on the night. Its eyelids swim
over human pupils. The heart of course

is many-ventricled, and the chambers beat
in three directions at once—its three

muscles working at off-intervals so that
it appears a frenzied man pushes and pulls

from inside. His action feeds the stomach, organ
of appetite and the filial scene. The meal—

fat with memory—went down the gullet, a long
greased slide past the clapboard hideout

in the voice box. The heavy meal
is indigestible. I have nothing left

to hide, my pachyderm, and nothing to make
the family (still in their rooms) speak to me.

Oakland Work Crew

Dan said, My life is a nine with the hammer cocked,
chuckled, told of standing on a brown lawn
naked, three hundred pounds of pure Mick-Spic:
shooting at a Chevelle, tire marks on concrete.
Told how, *inside,* you heat a sharpened Bic
and a guy carves DannyBoy or Norteaño on your neck.

Prince pictured faint patterns on ceiling tiles
in his dreams and a pot with a ten in it when he finds
where color begins. He brought a picture: he's thirteen,
Liberia, wide smile, fatigues, kalishnikov
hugging his shoulder. Told of barefoot soccer,
running on bricks, the grace of a clean pass.

I'm worth more than someone I meet, Rich said,
then described his daughter, his girl, and ladies
here, there. He explained what it means to be
a baldhead, why, if he sees a Sudeaño on Third,
he can't be held responsible what'll happen.
Told us which old school Cutlass' is hella tight.

Larry kept saying, High as an Oaktown sky,
that's all he said, aside from claiming vines
or brush or poison oak we cut and pulled
were a J with a hit so big he'd vanish. Never
told us what we knew: clapboard house,
cracked talk, brothers to keep in shoes.

And I went home and wrote a lover, told
how far hills were no matter where I drove,
how I didn't know what it was to be a tatted
baldhead, raise kids, play barefoot in the street,
one eye on the hammer, one ear to the barrel,
hearing a seashell inside the chamber.

Worry Bone

Woke gnawing its remains. Air
the brackish tinge of depths I had

all night been swimming in. No bird
song from the vine-covered fence

my room looks out on—not even
the pigeons' manic calls. I talked

myself down from the bed, a loft,
took paper in trade for the splintered

bone—human or animal
I don't know. I'd picked it clean though,

chewed the joint, cracked one end,
sucked the marrow. Tell me,

Mind, why you ravaged this limb-part.
Tell me what its owner told you in the dark.

Notes on Thirty Years
in the Life of a Ventriloquist

1974, Somewhere in the Midwest

First smile disguises gas.
Stuffed bear cries for milk.

1975–1976

Begin the sound of flowing water,
begin words of the toes.

First Soliloquies, 1977–1980

Often a redstart in the boneset and spotted knapweed.
Everything talks to me.

1981

Inimitable powers.
Exit father

1982, Normal, IL

Early studies with the master
necromancer, W. T. Moncrief.
Mother is skilled in sales
and the kind of smile—
lips open but not turned up,
eyes not crinkled—that is
its own accomplishment.

Realization, 1983

There are words one cannot say,
letters to be avoided.

1984

First major scar: closed
mouth on the left hand.

Lessons from the School Talent Show, 1985

Speaking is a kind of listening.
One hand must learn deception
while the other plays the innards.

1986–1987

Malarkey and bog-rot in parachute pants, then
a girl named Sweet Distraction.

First Job Interview, 1988

Can you juggle rings of fire?

I can throw my voice through rings of fire.

Kids like the rings, know what I mean?

*I can make dancing bears sing
as a girl juggles rings of fire.*

So you can't do the rings?
                                        No.
Thing is, nobody wants to listen
to a dummy. Plus, your lips move.

World Tour 1989

Cairo, Illinois to Denmark, Maine.
I'm never going home.

1990 New Year's Resolution, Whereabouts Unknown

No more hebetudinous frippery
or hell-bent chicanery.

1991, Fergus Falls

The Art of Forgetting
the Art of Speaking Plainly.
More sleight of hand.

Early '90s, Travels with the Circus

Two magicians (the one who swallowed a live piranha at five
and the one with room for acres of oranges in his lungs)
play their night orchestra on ash cans and bed springs.

Dressing Room Soliloquy, Las Vegas, 1994

In Gary, Indiana once—
the day's sulfur still
settling a thin sheen over all
of us—I left the audience

sniffling and puddling for more.
I wanted them somehow
clean. Such easy strings. I laughed
until I couldn't breathe.

1996

Divination by finger ring, divination
by the flight and cries of birds.

Fact, 1998

Among organs, the larynx has the highest ratio of nerve to
muscle fibers.

Bad Ideas of the Past Century

Southern Comfort in the green room.
Bent retching in Bend, Oregon.
O Sweet Distraction.

Post-Show Soliloquy, Kansas City, 2001

...On the same tour, Champagne had
townies who booed me off:
I'd been fixed on a woman
in pearls and gold lamé—

standing, staring. Most times,
I make them laugh, then listen
to what they say: *That* is a man
in perfect control. Those nights

I'm in the dressing room a little
later, shivering in front
of a black mirror. There's a toll
and that's not all of it.

Acquired Wisdom of 2002

...He found that, in proportion, as the strength of his
assumed voice increased, that of his natural voice
diminished.
—*The Life and Adventures of Valentine Vox*, 1840.

Unemployment Line, 2003

The tongue muscle wants
tooth-lip sambas, verbal pyrotechny.
The feet want flip-flops.

Pub Soliloquy in Zero, Iowa, Spring, 2004

You get to the point of wanting
your lips never to move,
to the point of whispers
pulsing and blurring on their own.

I went to see my mom in her home—
years since I saw her face—
and kept slipping into routines
as she spoke. My face held

its practiced smirk, from somewhere deep
the throat muttered its then
best lines. Together, she said,
we might make a person.

The End of Reading

A tingle, then the brush fire
in the limbic system.

A string of words, a sentence

It finds the zipper enclosing
your spine, and pulls.

I'm cold

Can you stare at the sparking?
Which strand might you peel from which

bundle and tie around your wrist before slipping
the whole thing back in?

Remember how it goes?

Will it slither back
inside its armor on its own?

I can't be walking around like this

A true author neither
apologizes nor gives a roadmap.

The ganglia won't let me loose

It is up to you, dear reader
to determine whether the work

will change your views,
prescription, habits.

Ever examined one of these things?

The reader and the text
together make a third thing.

I've grown a new lateral horn

Learning to Wait

I want to write an elegy to the edge of shade
in Spanish I almost understand, strange trills and clucks of
    tongue;

a sestina for the repeating ellipses of branches blown into
    dance;

a mambo ballad that's been tuning its chords in twitches
of fingers that don't pluck a note but know their tone and
    bend,

like murmuring banks where smiles from far-off tables
rise to meet needles and fall into the wind of a creek.

I want a sonnet for the place between your thighs,
the jeweled quiet there, the margins of that space,
like warmth of a dream you're just conscious of but haven't
    left yet;

I want to hold the line, to say: Here. Stop.

And point to bark of eucalyptus, late fall,
returning to leaves, cracking to speak a last flame of day
in a curling, slow sun, so dry it can only mouth its ending.

Inspiration

Ye blind guides, which strain at a gnat,
and swallow a camel. —Matthew 23:24.

Sudden as the swoop that lifts
from grass at once, a flash
of white under-feathers in sun—
follow its path, watch the landing
and scribble down the thumping
in your throat—find where *swallow*

began: its tiny muscles of flight
that link in our mouths to Philomel,
Puffer fish, blood of Christ.
Not the sugar-fed metaphor
sipped from a goblet, no,
metal and salt, tasted from the brow.

Fact is you swallow the lure,
hook and cackle—projected self,
protected—and learn your part
so well words rise from the low gullet
before you can wish them off.

A tire bobs near where water
disappears under limestone,
swallowed by earth, and Job
stands next to a pit he can't
see the bottom of. He tried
to force the camel down:

fur, femur, and teeth. And the drunks
in your family—they thought
swallowing seven mugs a night
was a way to forget; they forgot
each ounce enters the blood,
each sip leaves evidence.

Then there is the Black Swallower
prowling for fish twice
its size, which it downs by opening
a hinge and pulling the prey
in with teeth. It swallows
to cause its own splitting.

American Beech

Pimp-Daddy, Blow Me, and *D-Z 4-ever*
the only legible phrases, but other cuts

mark the squat trunk with hieroglyphs,
dark rings of hearts, snowflakes, arrowtips.

To be pocked like this. To stand in a corner
with shallow roots, one deep tap; to take

the terror-etchings, the fleeting love-wounds
onto skin and hold them out for someone

to see the blurred, healing edges and faint
unknowable letters. Despite the knife,

despite withering, to push an annual
dying farther, faster, and let anyone
anyone know this record of ache.

Ventriloquist on an Off-Day

Tucked in felt cases, his quiet ones sleep
the sleep of carved wood—he walks unknown

parks and blocks. Just happy to be here,
he says, bearing the city air: rainwater, soot.

He doesn't search for better ways to fool
an audience
                 or an oriole in summer weeds.

No journey back for youth's sea glass
or the seven thumping castles of bachelordom—

so much desire then he could taste a current
scoring the air between him and the other bodies.

The pull of it would recall his hand
on a van der Graaf machine at school:

each hair on end.
                 It's the same now

except he leans into the charged fields
with no designs on their end. And

the arcing currents that will not dissipate
beat all day beside his actual heart.

2

Panic Grass and Feverfew

After a quiet flash: a second sun
rose and fell and flattened four square miles—

half-grown potatoes cooked in the earth,
odd-shaped shadows burned on stones—

twelve days later,
                wildflowers would overtake
the epicenter's remains.
                     Sickle-senna

ruled next to goosefoot and yellow-eyed
bluets; Spanish bayonets and morning glories
near hairy-fruited bean. Broad green
with mealy-white undersides, sword-like
leaves, stubby white rays, climbing vines,
pea-flowers enclosed in burs with hooked spikes:

a field stood swaying, where houses had been.
Neck-high wildflowers, where houses had been.

Phaëton

It's different now. I've learned my lessons; I have
the helm. Aides place the crown, light, on my head.
Phoebus sits on a fence in a western state

watching steers chew green nubs to mud. You see,
I was born again, and took the throne to make
improvements. Who says a sun-king should sweat

through his robes behind the winged fire-steeds?
My cabinet is loyal and bright. Vulcan made
the chariot. New threats these days, new tests.

Some—I can't believe—doubt the sun, say
they'd live without it, and pray the opposite way.
Some make their own light. They don't understand

neutrinos, radiation dancing through us;
they'd ignore a gaze two million degrees
at center. Taps and polygraphs enlighten

our words and actions. I tell the Hours, Relax,
we have crack teams to harness the steeds' chest-fire
and blazing breath. We know how to stir plasma,

focus rays. Evildoers must be made
to see. Bent to the big picture. We have
emergency plans; I'll govern from a cave.

God's been informed the fire may singe the planet.
I've imparted the importance. If He can't arrange
our safety, we'll do it ourselves. Tell those people

their day of liberation is here: we'll part
the waters; enemies will bow in shock and awe.
We're a peaceful people, wielding a god-size fireball.

Ventriloquist on the Moor

The ladder in his throat
rungless, greased. His voices—
unformed whimpers now—

twitch in his ears. He wanders
in a fog that stinks with wound-
wort and wonders how long

his body will last when he lies
down in the peat. Will he
decay once for each of them

or become bones in days—
organs proving empty
but for the voices' carrion

inside his lungs? His lips
splinter. His chest clatters.
His heart is not his own.

Still Life, Young Woman
at the Water's Edge

You tell yourself you won't need to lean—
falling is the last thing
                    you want to do.
You tell yourself you don't want rapids' fury
of sound and rock, slate shelf, quartz edge,
blur of reeds and what stirs in eddies.
                                    You tell
yourself you don't want to study the pull
of eel grass winding your ankles.
                            It could be
Lethe's black water asking you to drink
at daybreak, or the Winooski's snowmelt—
a peculiar high note as it rounds a bend.
Back away.
                You're not a willow branch.
Take off your garland of crow-flowers, nettles,
creeping vines. The water will not hesitate to
close over you.
                    It will keep on, somnolent
promise of flow. Don't tell yourself you want
to see the reflection of your face
                            even once.

Park City Grille

After John Currin: oil on canvas, 2000

Caught in mid-titter, not meeting
his gaze, chin tipped, she lets him study her

true prize, the neck he calls long,
elegant. It lengthens before his eyes, a mile

of pale skin lit by platinum locks.
Her bone-thin arm brings a hand to his lap

under the table; he wonders if
his coat's walnut suede, which matches his hair,

clinched it. Or did the place—rustic
chairs, mountain wildflowers, a simple vase—

make him sincere? Who cares. The neck
continues to lengthen: a claret amaryllis

so intent on meeting light it would
tear its bulb out of earth, tip the pot

by leaning. I can't stop them and can't
stop looking. Someone make him feel

his touch; make her feel her turning
off-center—she's smiling, letting him push.

A Brief History of the Decline

1. The Summation

I began this trial with a list: leaf-spines,
the quivering inside fox-sparrow wings,
a little girl in a blue dress who rides

her bicycle through a mist, roadside lupine,
black-eyed susans, a bottle-nosed dolphin
leaping and arcing in a boat's wake.

Ladies and gentlemen, the eyes pass off
surfaces as attractive depth. They have us
believing every other person on the street

is the rarest Junonia or lightning whelk.
As I've said, each and every glimpse contains
some arsenic. I've told you the tragic tale

of symphonies a writer had to hold
in mind to keep his eyes from steak knives.
I've cited azurite and banded jasper,

the only objects known to slow their wants.
Over and again, I've proved the eyes
go where the gilt and curve direct.

2. After the Sentencing

At first, they wandered, blind,
and wondered at the paraffin, rosemary,
leaf rot, and sweet almond
oil, nosed as if for the first time. Sidewalks
were gauntlets of fingers—
all of them came to know each other anew.
They heard the small hands
of oak leaves. Fondled the dewed grass.
Attended to. The tongue
became a multi-purpose organ: taste,
touch, and sight. Time was told by heat.

3. Overheard at a Local Tavern

I'm telling you the sex was great. Better
than ever. Like we figured out a new
blind geometry.

    ....

             I don't know, it's just
a talent I have—I use my hands to see.

    ....

Listen, I thought you wanted to hear this.

    ....

For weeks there was this hum to how she talked.

    ....

Her note said, Everything has changed.
I can't read your face anymore.

4. Months Later, the Lawyer Returned

So much night errantry. All is
jagged-edged. Where are my Klieg lights, my spot-lamps, my
    gadabouts—

tufthunters, louts. Re-dice: let me
throw them again, this time back in. Let me tell it all again.

Make me a honey drudger
once more. I miss thinking I've seen the Nereids: Master's
    Lovely Consort,

Never-Wrong, Bounty-of-the-Deep.
I can't find the jar of sorrows even, the pocketful of god, the
    muse

once found stuttering in folds of coast:
granite and metamorphic quartz and mica.
                       Now nothing can save me.

Nothing can shame me. I've brewed
oolong and umlaut to no avail. Railroad ties would make
    good tongues.

I'd give all four senses, all this
scratchiti, for one minute of the sweet deaths and quick
    tinctures of sight.

The Origin of Pigeons

After Ovid

Two lovers—at once afire, smothered—
couldn't quit their love, or sex, even
when separate, and cried, *Spasms!*
I love you, psalms!, until the voices
they began to use with each other,
say, walking down the street
for more milk and a video, and even,

after a while, the voices they tried
on others, were the pleasure-tinged
proclamations of the boudoir.
One of the minor gods, just then
stalled over an epic next door,
grew furious with the noise and left them
with this quieter arc of former cries,

like a muffled, good jazz that loops
back to find a new cadence for touch
and never gets it, that final purr,
even at sunrise. The birds cooing
in my eaves come from those first two
who chirred to concrete cliffs, and their
raptures never slacken, never conclude.

One of the Dummies at Night

He slept in the tinder box
his master made, and oak
grain governed the dreaming—

his left eye clouded over,
he closed the other and saw
mild applause in his future.

His bed sat at a crevice
edge, pure pitch below,
and a cold wind slowed

the senses, rising from who
knows where. Later his mind
became its pin, eschewed

dowels and string and leapt
into the dark. The fall
was pleasurable, apt:

there were no voices
in the breeze, no speeches
to open his mouth.

3

Explanation Beginning with a River

Swimming in a thin print dress among piranhas—
that year, you learned a place I can't fathom.

In a jungle three thousand miles away, you
watched sea turtles hide their eggs in the dark;

you gathered bitter cassavas, drained their poison
for days to make bread.

                            You have patients now:
a woman drips with toxins, a guy in a johnny
chases you down the hall
                                cursing for opiates.

You have this place you go to:

I can shake the sky for nighthawks and parse

the bark-puzzle of a London Plane. It doesn't
matter how many other people I talk to:

at home, I listen to the pipes knock inside
our walls. I don't know how to be alone.

Maker

Did he smile his work to see?

Once the ventriloquist had finished
the dummy—buffed the pine nose,
tested the mouth action, sewed
the little tuxedo coat—

he heard a voice. He often found
the way a dummy would speak
by sitting with it. But this tone
and cadence were his own.

(This isn't a story in which
the dummy slips out at night
and holds a pillow to
his maker's face.) Numbness

comes—slack, dull— when a voice
you thought yours leaves you
and you confuse an audience
with a room full of empty chairs.

Wildflowers of North America

I was there on the phone with my wrench (a mistflower:
tiny clusters of violet fuzz)
when all you wanted was the cave of my right ear.

Even knotweed and three-leaf clover know how
to listen. And a woodland sunflower: it twists

and cranes stalk and disc—see, there I go again.
I should be wishing that the thirty-year-old mother

and wife, your patient, survive the non-native villages
that colonize her organs like ragweed or ivy

(those rows of green nodding heads,
that creeping, sun-diminishing death).

I should have said, Let that invasion be overrun
with blackberry thickets and jewelweed
(good thorns; a burst of orange, seedpods that pop).

I should have said, I'll be home soon, love, leave
your white coat anywhere you want. A sudden field:

I'll be your Lobelia and Coreopsis. I swear
(petals like little lips and ears, scent of anise)
I thought the names could make things better.

Self-Portrait as a Word Ending in E

Tell me why certain kinds of noise—
wood snapping to embers, a river's drift—always bring ease.

You know me: the lone guy screaming inside
his car in traffic, snapping so easily out of ease.

Last night I knocked over a handmade vase
(wedding present, another hundred pieces) with such ease.

Hugged a rock ledge, crawled under a pine
and found the long path gives its own sore, wet, and splayed ease.

Sleep fits too much breath into too little
space—it's painful to listen to a body fight for ease.

Ask me if I know what clatters inside
the line; a rhythm brings the mental hamster to its ease.

I'll never know what causes the noise—
crazy white man, son of some Gilbert, always in need of ease.

Notes on Colic

The trouble is / that a cry eludes form.
—*Zbigniew Herbert*

1. Lullaby of His Second and Third Months

I'm not a patient person. (Repeat)
Please, please fall asleep.
No stars tonight, no moon.
Let's wipe that milk from your top lip.

You've heard by now about the stars
I know: holes in sackcloth,
light bugs on hooks, or dead stars'
old light. No one has set a path

for us, or will, but us.
Try the magic blanket schtick
if it helps you close your eyes.
I'll be right here, my face lamplit.

2. Continuous Crying, Date Unknown

After I punched a wall
I felt better. The bricks
didn't blink, of course. My right

bled a little, my left
throbbed its sympathy.
Don't tell me the physical

can't stand in for what
I wished to hit. The beauty
of stoicism is never

having to say exactly.
One lets the momentary
act—the clench, the swing—

stand in for depth of feeling.
It's a particular kind
of courage, of cowardice

to train yourself to watch
the look on your face, not
the blood pulsing behind it.

3. Dream

The foreman of the pity factory,
where they produce the tiniest
violins known to man—the newest

model fits under a fingernail
and is played by blowing on
the hand in question—that guy,

who can't stop itching his welts,
who rushes home to wash
his wife's and mother-in-law's

undergarments, nightly,
who accidentally taught
his son a jet-engine

whine, who can't recall
sex, ever, does a little jig
to make you feel better.

How to Make Fatherhood Lyrical

I could describe the arc of piss
as *sanctifying* the changing table

or argue that his wailing resembles
a certain style of opera—

one develops a taste for its peaks
as evidence of proper training,
the cultivation of a gift.

I might tell you that when the dog
tugs the leash in one direction

and the stroller rolls in the other
it's similar to the push and pull

of family and vocation, and each
in turn alters its course.

Surely I'd research and touch on
why gerbils eat their young

and moose will charge if you dare step
between mother and calf.

But none of this is the truth
I tell myself or don't,
depending on the morning:

it's not a set of lyrics, it's prose—
as in pedestrian, a man

on foot, not some freak stallion,
not a Clydesdale, not even a draft—

and every day I have to choose
whether to write myself in.

Music in My Head

I don't want news this morning
                            I don't even want my son
(just past one) not to cry
                    a little when I drop him off

This cold clear blue I'll take, endless color
                                And the maple
up the street, already gone past green
                        A mess of reds

fired in a night kiln
                    Each a shade that will become
different tomorrow
                    Whoever's responsible for this

made it
        so we don't have to believe anyone or thing
did
        and, today, all the little lambs in the wood know

there's no one who can watch over
                            who can be
the one, because a one—Was there
                            ever a one?

Made by whom?
            Who makes a maker you don't have to believe
except a one
            who can't possibly see how to watch over me

Death of a Ventriloquist

It happens off stage, off
page, off-ed—not by
voices, not by a dummy—

by the sound of no
one, no clapping, nothing
said or to say, empty

vessel. Crash victims
can learn to speak again.
Can this one learn how

to listen? He'd better, better
not be dead—his son
(now four) crawls into bed.

4

Proof #4

One never says exactly what one means.
One does not know what it is to mean, except

when finding the quotient of the sum of some
numbers divided by the number of them.

The mean of sparrow and swallow is marrow.
If one adds hope to the equation, it becomes

harrow. Still, one and one and one is still
a fallow addition. To swallow a sparrow

is my only hope. To watch for sweetspire
in a meadow, knowing my chances are narrow.

Visiting Chicago

The same high, pointed fences guarding nothing
I want. The same flat spill that says I will

lie down at the slightest flinch. This is new, this
reaching to admit a subway run through me.

If the lake will have me. If the lake will let me
say, this was home. Wadded, tooth-marked, dried,

the tilled word insists on its tiny flavor.
My kind of town, it says, My kind of city,

hacking up a lung. My El, my pallor, my gas-
fed water, tell me how to touch your walks.

Remember how to swim? it says, Do you still
know how to save someone and not drown?

Four Planes of Experience

1. Reception & Contemplation

Whenever I walk the dog at dusk,
a certain silence of breath. Hitch-knot
over an ear. My split condition:

always cleaving, taking leave.
The branches' synaptic map, a wind
within the wind. Two sawhorses

say Fire & Rescue—how about
no fire, no retinue needed?
The maple that drops its green

rather than submit to a long
fall: preventative. At a certain age,
certain slow-growth cancers occur

in all patients. To consider this
stand of pines is to will a screech
owl who wakes at dusk to hunt

its limits, the word *pine* a home
calling in the shadow of its beak.
Who hasn't wished for greater returns

from Benefits Services agents?
Of course the hours proceed like this,
fingers along suspicious moles,

the splitting veins. Someone I know
calls her hours of insomnia
solving the problems of the world.

When I say *world*, I mean distance:
me on one bank, you on the other,
a rushing between that could be fire.

When I say *fire*, I mean
a slash and burn, ash circling
in the black willows, a singing.

2. As It Happened Narration

The dog (impatient, loafing) drops his ball
and drops his ball and, sick of my staring, eats
the millipedes that crawl out of the closet,
where they are fucking and fucking nightly.

I decide to take the dog for a walk
and, as we enter the park, think,
I bet this buffel grass was planted above
a trove of fossils and graves, which is right

about when I see the five screech owls unfurl
and stretch. Long-lost cousins of the hawk,
dusk hunters, they sweep through the willows, scan
a field of asters and the gristle weeds.

3.1. Recall: Nostalgia

The sun had been the perfect past
of sun, before the earth was peopled and unpeopled and light
    coursed through its valley of hours
and fell with matches and withering.

From the blockhouse lookout,
the ice rink sank its love songs into the hills around, and the
    elms, locusts, and hornbeams
were listening, each grove
switching, each tousled branch sifting north wind up along
    the paths running their tracks,
cement and sand—all
these songs converging on
the old house of stone.

Like any spring, the molting
everywhere made eyewells pulse. Often nothing stayed still so
    I would stand until I could
separate clicking squirrels
from seed pods falling on slate.

I recall you weren't there
and the dog was, but when I saw the owls and heard their
    machine whirrs, I remembered we were
both early adults, two
children who could talk to adults because they know that
    bodies (hamster, human) will stiffen—
eight shushed in a year.

3.2. Recall: A Note on False Memories

Atoms are not things, they are tendencies. Particles can be
in multiple places at once—easier for a mind to fix them, say,
at the park, having an epiphany. It is true at the sub-nuclear
level we can be understood to be one: *owls, pines, you, I.*
It is also true that addictions, say, to solitary revellings, are
possible because we have dreamt of nothing better.

3.4. Recall: Gaps in the Record

Around that time I was reading things like:
The knights in the wood knew the moon never
would cure their supersensual loneliness,
and writing things like: Once in a while I let
go of the brake, the late night conductor

said easily. Or was that a previous spring?

4. Recording

No logical system is free
from inconsistency. If one
has reeked of box wine, one
knows this, or if you've had
the woods stuck in your eye.

Add to that that nothing existent
is measurable except
by slight collisions and flitterings
imperceptible to senses,
Henry Adams said, more or less.

This is not to speak of facts
(gilt-trimmed talons, for instance)
left out. The issue with the you:
she's not the she exactly—more
a sum of missing gears.

In *Minimalism Simplified*
Einstein says *now* depends on where
you stand. Thus for the you
who has a bulse of flints always
on her person, the one

here and not here, who listens
to her old patients rattle
on for hours and listens
to her old man rattle on

on owls and all the missing letters:
I is such a narrow one,
so singular, so flimsy,
but *we* still means enough.

Rattling Funicular

The pleasure of insomnia
(after its right jab to the jaw)

is it renders the quiet world again:
there is the stoplight that flashes

a dead street all night. Here lie
two boys—one, splayed, dreams

of head-butting his mother
and a misshapen paper heart's

Izzy in slanted scrawl. The other
curls into his bed, words

tumbling, leaping, skittering through
his mind the way they'll rise

later in his mouth—each a new
twirl, tang, tintinnabulation,

never thought-through—his tongue
moves as if someone holds

its strings. That's what this is too:
something tugs at my little rope

and my rust begins to inch
a slope. Where does this drive

come from? Insert sleeplessness.
Insert throat-narrowing rage. Insert

calm that spreads through bones
like heat and words that appear

sometimes out of the solid ice
new, warm, and crystalline.

Caravaggio's Peter

Firelight reveals the mire
in a woman's eyes,

makes a soldier all shadow,
all stance and hand,

unfurls each furrow
and taut line in Peter's face:

clench of eyes, rock
liquefying in the corners.

I'm burning my doctrines.
I want to forgive him.

The center of everything

is the mouth, silent, open,
done saying what cannot be

unsaid—two words burnt
on the voice box: *Not me.*

The Prayer of Glass

1

Let the clattering engine with an undetectable crack
quit its rib-rattling racket. Let the infant's fever

break easily as a stick split over a knee,
one end thrown for a puppy, the other pitched.

Let the neighborhood children play with sticks
without taking them to each other's bodies.

Let the small bird some of us still carry
inside our bones remain a small bird, not

a pigeon or hook-beaked gull or whippoorwill,
(the names we learn confuse the fact that

sometimes bird is bird) and let its bones
be whole no matter how many times we forget

to put a little bird sticker on the glass patio door
because there is a part of us—okay, me—in corners

of certain organs, that likes to say, Oh, you poor poor
thing, and touch a tiny quivering wing.

It'll be alright. There's a part of us
that likes to think that all will be right, as if

that were a matter of glass doors and tiny bird
stickers and rust-riddled mufflers in the upper chest

that keep right on coughing after the engine stops.
You're fine, you're okay, I tell my son whenever he falls

testing his unfused skull plates on a wood floor
or rock or road and he'll lie there for a second

looking up at me. And whether he smiles a little
and gets back up or begins a wail that crests

over the whole backyard, he has, up to this point,
been fine, which means I haven't lied to him.

2

At least not any of the big, look-you-
in-the-eyes whoppers that you spend a life

or two trying to figure out. I didn't want this
to be about my father. How many times

has that kind of engine stalled an otherwise
serviceable vehicle? How many hours over

how many years have I spent listening
to the way ice clinking in his glass

promised its opposite: solidity and certainly
no sheriff knocking on the door. How many

minutes have I spent staring into the vast
unnameable region beneath the hood?

I can't even tell you what a carburetor
does, where the timing is, or how to manage

an oil pan. A scrub jay hides behind
lilacs—the way it limp-thrashes scares me.

Let this be so: when there comes a kind
of truth to tell—your bird and my bird hurtle

toward it—even if I have to shut a glass door
I tell you. As if the saying could make it so.

Disabused Sonnet

Disconnected, disaffected, dissed
by my own flesh and blood, i.e.
me. Here's the hissing rain again
disappointing by appointing the walks
with lakes and swift rivers in miniature.
I've missed this sound; I've dismissed
the quiet disproportionate and scarce.
Your central muscle is undisclosed
and mine undiscovered, undone, un-
determined. It's true
we disafforested to the point
of dirt, we disanointed
with bleach—we wanted little
disagreement and woke left with this.

The Perhaps World

In one I like to tell, I'm quartz
and humble but still see into

the leaded forest. I read the intricate
fingerwork of bare cherry trees and place

my ear to soil, never doubting that hum.
In another, I wake inside a pile of leaves

filmed and blank. I know no wind
or rocks or earth. The faces of my sons

and my love appear—if I could
remember their names, I'd know the way.

In still another world, bills titter
on shelves and green bottles whisper

through keyholes. The great lost
opus lies on the couch scratching its belly.

If I could triangulate, if I could
conjure—how many worlds would it take

to circumscribe and name this white sky,
this sizzle of rain, this diesel in my chest?

Pull

When I say I'll never grasp
how he could loop a rope
around his neck and step
off a chair, I mean it

makes me sick. I mean
anyone—how could you
do it? There's always one
who really believes you

will stay and now she will
never believe her own
gut again. In the game
the poets like to fool

with at parties, like charades
with wine, you have to guess
which writer he is and how
he off-ed himself. Is he

Levi heaving his own
body down the stairs,
or Plath, a towel, an oven,
her kids behind the door?

I understand the rain
when it's relentless: salt
water up to the lip
of the wharf parking lot.

The rocks wait for a man
to fill his pockets with them
and walk into that flat
water like he's walking

to pick up more milk.
There are tethers: a love,
two boys who look at me
and believe, and one morning

I might write something
sharp and worth keeping.
Some days there is this pull.
I said a man, not me.

The Worst First Line

I'm happy
can sometimes be redeemed
because the midnight house is made
from breath and electric quiet;

because particulate matter
in the atmosphere allows
a particular inhuman crimson
to appear;

because the toddler wouldn't nap
but did lie down for a whole hour
singing about a race he'd run
someday;

because the baby has us
sleepless, the boy has us
breathless and minutes ago
I carried

him upstairs while he screamed;
because I held him by one
arm and one leg and he
was kicking

and I knew I was close
to hurting him. I knew
if I let my mind go I
would hurt him.

With you and the two boys
in the room I say, I know
you're not happy. Because your face
almost breaks.

Because male bumblebees
look armed, terrifying,
but never sting—their stingers
evolved

into genitals that grip
the queen for over an hour,
and she can even fly
him somewhere;

because, after Taps, Big
Campfire, and Hush Little Baby,
my son turns to me, says, Are
you happy?

More Matter, Less Art

As a sycamore on 104th
makes plastic bags fettered to limbs

into garments of muslin and wind,
so have you filled me with holes.

As a fox sparrow under a hedge
behind a fence twits and prets

and goes unnoticed, so have your
small touches worked into my fourth

ventricle an unspoken chorus
I can't call up and can't forget.

I forgot to tell you when you left
how I swallowed you while we slept—

not as in the throat, as in
the bird, its unsung note.

The Nots

*A writer is accountable also for what
he chooses not to write. —Edmond Jabés*

I haven't described the flight path of my shouts
at two toddlers in a car. I've said little

of my father, a dash. I've not been head
in hands, unable to stop my baby's wails.

That wasn't me, slack-jawed before a screen,
vacant as neon, forgetting my own name.

Not once have I forgotten my son
on his birthday or how to touch my wife.

That was someone else who tightened
your heart with a skate key. Confessed not

being the cherry atop a Manhattan,
nor a tiny umbrella crinkling over a daiquiri.

No tantrums on or off the page.
I told none of the stories I wished to.

They turned out to be tangles of nerve fibers
unjoined, two roads without a bridge between.

I've not spread my arms wide as they would
and said, *Do with me what you will.*

Notes

Both "Rider Unhorsed" and "Ventriloquist on the Moor" were written after sketches by Paul Klee.

The first line of "Guide" is adapted from Longfellow's translation of the *Inferno*.

The italicized line in "The Origin of Pigeons" is the first line of an untitled Paul Celan poem in the McHugh-Popov translation.

"Panic Grass and Feverfew" takes its inspiration from the John Hersey essay "Hiroshima," which first appeared in *The New Yorker* in 1946.

The structure of "Four Planes of Experience" owes a debt to James Agee's *Let Us Now Praise Famous Men*.

Praise for Previous Winners of the
Vassar Miller Prize in Poetry

Circles Where the Head Should Be, by Caki Wilkinson:

"Playful and soulful, buoyant and mordant, snazzy and savvy—Caki Wilkinson's poems pull out all the stops, and revel in making the old mother tongue sound like a bright young thing. Lend her your ears and you'll hear American lyric moxie in all its abounding gusto and lapidary glory, making itself new all over again."—David Barber, Poetry Editor, *The Atlantic*

"*Circles Where the Head Should Be* has its own distinctive voice, a lively intelligence, insatiable curiosity, and a decided command of form. These qualities play off one another in ways that instruct and delight. An irresistible book."—J. D. McClatchy, author of *Mercury Dressing: Poems,* judge

"Caki Wilkinson's marvelous and marvelously titled *Circles Where the Head Should Be* contains poetry as dexterously written as any today. And beneath its intricate surface pleasures lie a fierce intelligence and a relentless imagination constantly discovering connections where none had been seen before. This is a stunning debut."—John Koethe, author of *Ninety-fifth Street*, winner of the Lenore Marshall Prize

"Like Frost, Wilkinson believes in poem as performance, showing off her verve and virtuosity. She is the 'Lady on a Unicycle,' negotiating her difficult vehicle through the pedestrian crowd with 'the easy lean achieved/ by holding on to nothing'—a joy to witness." —A. E. Stallings, author of *Archaic Smile* and *Hapax*

———

77

Stray Home, by Amy M. Clark:

Two poems from *Stray Home* were selected by Garrison Keillor, host of *A Prairie Home Companion* and of *The Writer's Almanac* to be included in *The Writer's Almanac*, broadcast May 28 and 29, 2010.

"*Stray Home* is a great read. The poetic form found in its pages never feels forced or full of clichés. Whether you are a fan of formal verse or just like to 'dabble,' *Stray Home* is a collection to pick up."—*Good Reads*

———

Ohio Violence, by Alison Stine:

"In the mind, Ohio and violence may not be words immediately paired—pastoral cornfields, football fields, and deer versus the blood and splintered bone of a fight or a death. Yet *Ohio Violence* achieves that balance of the smooth and vivid simmer of images and the losses that mount in Alison Stine's collection."—*Mid-American Review*

"Shot through with a keen resolve, *Ohio Violence* is an arresting, despairing book that alternately stuns and seduces."—*Rain Taxi*

"One comes away from *Ohio Violence* newly impressed with the contingency and instability of the hazardous universe that is our home; and impressed, as well, with the ability of these stark, memorable poems to distill that universe into language and to make of it a sad and haunting song."—Troy Jollimore, *Galatea Resurrects #13*

———

Mister Martini, **by Richard Carr:**

"This is a truly original book. There's nothing extra: sharp and clear and astonishing. Viva!"—Naomi Shihab Nye, author of *Fuel,* judge

————

The Next Settlement, **by Michael Robins:**

"Michael Robins' prismatic poems open windows, then close them, so we're always getting glimpses of light that suggest a larger world. With never a syllable to spare, these poems are beautiful and haunting. I know of nothing like them."—James Tate, winner of the 1992 Pulitzer Prize for Poetry

"*The Next Settlement* is a finely honed, resonant collection of poems, sharp and vivid in language, uncompromising in judgment. The voice in this book is unsparing, often distressed, and involved in a world which is intrusive, violent, and deeply deceitful, where honesty and compassion are sought for in vain, and refuges for the mind are rare." —Anne Winters, author of *The Key to the City,* judge

————

re-entry, **by Michael White:**

"Michael White's third volume does what all good poetry does: it presents the sun-drenched quotidiana of our lives, and lifts it all into the sacred space of poetry and memory. He delights us with his naming, but he also makes us pause, long enough at least to take very careful stock of what we have. He makes us want to hold on to it, even as it trembles in the ether and dissolves."—Paul Mariani, author of *Deaths and Transfigurations,* judge

"Here is a book that explores the interplay between interior and exterior landscapes with such generous and beautifully crafted detail that readers will feel they are no longer reading these poems but living them."—Kathryn Stripling Byer, Poet Laureate of North Carolina 2005–2009

"In Michael White's latest opus, figure after figure emerge from chaotic ground of memory, such verdant upswellings an urgent music pressured up from deep wells before subsiding—high waterlines left in our wake to mark the turbulence of love's intractable flood." —Timothy Liu, author of *For Dust Thou Art*

The Black Beach, by J. T. Barbarese:

"*The Black Beach* constantly delights with its questing, surprising, and not-easily-satisfied imagination. But simultaneously it creates an exacting and exhilarating vision of 'God, the undoer that does.' The speaker who, in one poem, stands in the moment 'love/what is not,' is the same one who, in another poem, imagines 'the black beach of heaven where all desire/ is merged, twinned, recovered, braided, and set ablaze.'"—Andrew Hudgins, author of *Ecstatic in the Poison*, judge

"A dark brilliance shines in these honed, memorable poems of the human predicament: that of a sentient particle with a mind for the infinite. 'Looking for meaning/ the way radio waves sought Marconi,' Barbarese's restless imagination searches through the stations of the daily to the 'very end of the dial/ the static that never signs off,' and turns back to receive what we have, the 'lonely surprised heart/ shaken. . .'"—Eleanor Wilner, author of *The Girl with Bees in Her Hair*

"Barbarese has an uncanny ability to size up the urban scene, then hallow and harrow it. Putting his daughter on the local train for the city, he conjures up those who rode in the box-cars to the ovens. And, leaning over 'winged rot . . . glued . . . to shat-on grass' in a nearby park, he can think 'how beauti-ful,/ the hard frost had cemented/ what had lived to what never did.' He wins me over in poem after poem."—Maxine Kumin, author of *The Long Marriage*

Losing and Finding, by Karen Fiser:

"There are so many delights in this book, interpenetrated by so many losses. . . . She keeps her eye unflinchingly on 'the rough loving arms of this world,' even as she is buffeted about by it."—Lynne McMahon, judge

"From the searing heart of pain and patience come the transporting poems of Karen Fiser. Trust them. Treasure them. These poems are resounding, important, and deeply humane."—Naomi Shihab Nye, author of *Fuel*

Bene-Dictions, by Rush Rankin:

"*Bene-Dictions* is a canny, unnerving book. Its cool manners seem to hold compassion at bay; but its irony is a cleansing discipline which allows it to conjure complex lusts, hurts, and injustices without self-pity and, apparently, without delusion. These poems describe a world in which 'Tenderness is an accident of character/ or energy, or just a side-effect/ of hav-ing failed at what you wanted,' but in which the reader, to read the effect of rain on paper, 'opens the book/ in a storm,

as though to find the world itself in tears.'"
—Rosanna Warren, judge

"If the long hours in offices of the mind elect for us mean-ingfulness, they must always eventually find the human heart. Then Rankin's vivid and surprising poems map that move-ment where as Rilke insists, what is sublime is mundane, and everything that falls must somehow in shadow/act, rise."
—Norman Dubie

———

The Self as Constellation, by Jeanine Hathaway:

"This is a collection to be read in sequence because the con-tinuity is powerful and persuasive. If we are attentive readers, we end like the nuns in the storm cellar 'not knowing wheth-er we've been struck by lightning or by love.'"—Madeline DeFrees, judge

———

The Perseids, by Karen Holmberg:

"It is a rare pleasure to encounter these days a young poet so thoroughly at home in the natural world, so deeply attuned to its mysteries, that reading her book we enter, in turn, that 'Spherical Mirror,' the elemental mind which, as *The Perse-ids* reminds us, forms 'the core of human bliss.'"—Sherod Santos, judge

———

A Protocol for Touch, by Constance Merritt:

"Merritt's prosodic range is prodigious—she moves in

poetic forms as naturally as a body moves in its skin, even as her lines ring with the cadenced authority of a gifted and schooled ear. Here, in her words, the iambic ground bass is in its vital questioning mode: 'The heart's insistent under-song: how live? // how live? How live?' this poetry serves no lesser necessity than to ask that."—Eleanor Wilner, author of *The Girl with Bees in Her Hair* and judge

---

Moving & St rage, by **Kathy Fagan**:

"Kathy Fagan's long awaited second collection keeps reveal-ing new strengths, new powers. Its words are of unsparing rigor; its intelligence and vision continually spring forward in changed ways. These are poems both revealing and resistant: deeply felt, deeply communicative, yet avoiding any easy lyri-cism. Again and again the reader pauses, astonished by some fresh turn of language, of insight, of terrain. *Moving & St rage* offers extraordinary pleasures, clarities, and depth." —Jane Hirshfield, author of *Come, Thief*

"From the first emblems of language—the angular letters of A and K—a child steps toward the preservation of conscious-ness, and, in turn, the paradox of preserving that which is lost. These beautifully crafted poems trace a journey to adult-hood and grief with a lyrical mastery that is breathtaking. What can language do with loss? Fagan asks. This splendid book is her answer."—Linda Bierds

---

Soul Data, by **Mark Svenvold**:

"*Soul Data* is rarely compounded—of wit and music, surface

elegance and intellectual depth, quirk and quandary. Its sensual intelligence is on high alert, and the sheer unsheerness of its language—all its densities and textures—is a linguiphilical delight. Unmistakably American (the poetry's occasions and its cadences alike serve for signature) it has the jinx-meister's humors about it. A fine rhetorical savvy, in a mind inclined to the chillier depths: among poetic gifts these days it's an uncommon conjunction, a gift of mysteries, like the sight (across a night pond's surface) of bright-blue shooting star: one hopes the other humans get to see it."—Heather McHugh, author of *Upgraded to Serious*

American Crawl, by Paul Allen:

"It is absolutely no exaggeration to say that no one is writing like Paul Allen. There is not an ounce of flab in his poems, which are informed by an urgency, a sense of personal commitment, and a passion rarely seen in contemporary poetry. America in the 1990s is not a comfortable world in which to live; and Paul Allen is certainly not the man to entertain us with fanciful invitations to dens of innocence. Though *American Crawl* is a first book, there is nothing jejune about the poems, or about the unique imagination that creates them. The publication of this book is an important contribution to American letters."—Richard Tillinghast, author of *The New Life*

The Sublime, by Jonathan Holden:

"*The Sublime* embodies a poetry that is personal and public, and shows through clear-cut imagery how varied our imagined and actual lives are. Everything seems to be woven into this ambitious collection: love, war, divorce, fear, anger, doubt, grace, beauty, terror, popular culture, nature. This poetry challenges us to remain (or become) whole in an increasingly fragmented world."—Yusef Komunyakaa, judge

---

Delirium, by Barbara Hamby:

"Barbara Hamby is an extraordinary discovery! A poet of compassion and elegance, she is a poet whose debut in *Delirium* promises a rich (and enriching) lifelong project." —Cynthia Macdonald, author of *Living Wills*

Partial Eclipse, by Tony Sanders:

"Sanders brings together his own sensibility (quizzical, approaching middle-age, slightly disaffected, bemused, learned but not stuffy) and an alertness to what can be appropriated from history, myth, the daily papers."—*Choice*

". . . a distinguished first collection from a poet about whom we will be hearing more."— *Houston Post*

"Sanders proceeds through his . . . poems with a pervasive steadiness of diction, . . . a syntactic resonance quite his own yet gratefully beholden to such exacting masters as Stevens and Ashbery. The freshness of the poems is a result of their immersion in life with others, achieving the resolute tonality of a man speaking not so much out or up but on, talking his way to the horizon."—Richard Howard, judge

CPSIA information can be obtained at www.ICGtesting.com
Printed in the USA
LVOW082230020212

266673LV00004BA/1/P